Dreamers
&
Doers
— in Business

Success & Failure in Small Business

Roger Alliman

Dedicated to the many
small business owners
who understand their product,
service, and industry
and are willing to learn more
about selecting
and working with the
right people
who can help them
toward success.

Contents

INTRODUCTION

Dreamers
&
Doers

Conducting the operations of a successful business can be gratifying, disappointing, and just plain mystifying.

Insiders confess that it takes a team effort to produce and sell a product or service successfully in today's hyper-competitive marketplace. Observers note the wide-scale need for strong management teams to guide and direct company efforts.

There are two primary leadership needs at the top

of any successful organization that provide a balance of direction. Those functions are expressed in the delicate tension between the visionary role *(the dreamer)* that keeps the creative process moving, and the activity functions *(the doer)* that exercise the fundamental principles of good business operation. These two powers are essential to any winning effort. As with any team effort, the game is, more often than not, won or lost with the proper lineup capable of providing those elements.

Most companies, small, medium, and large are driven by one of four recognizable sources:

- Personality - Nearly every metro area has a car dealer who does his own commercials using high-pitched, high pressure, and over-the-top gimmicks to offer you that once-in-a-lifetime deal. Everything about his dealership spins off his personality. Some franchises started with a personality-driven image to gain the public confidence. Notable are KFC's Colonel Sanders and Wendy's owner Dave Thomas.
- Product - Product-driven companies might include fast food establishments like Dairy Queen or McDonalds where the product is a known quantity. Another example might be a home product like Pella windows where the

image is product-driven.

• <u>Service</u> - Carpet cleaners, plumbers, and land-scapers fall into this category, thought of in terms of a service rather than product or personality.

• <u>Need</u> - These are businesses that fill a need from your local supermarket to your dentist or vet. They provide a necessary service and often location and availability that are their essential marketing assets.

The success of each of these companies depends on good management. There must be visionary ideas culminating in sound aggressive goals. There must also be task-centered organization that brings the goals to the daily task at hand.

In nearly every company, there is a tendency at the top to limit the company focus to the gifting of the top executive. He is bent on focusing the decision making process through the paradigm of his talent and skill. As a result, a large portion of the decisions will often be made through the processing skills of his template.

Subsequently, a company may take on the personality and feed on the direction of "the top," regardless of the competence or ability to provide balanced direction in both of the key areas essential to success — dreaming and doing.

Finding a balance of these two vital ingredients should be the management goal of every company, large or small. Although there have been, and are, a few men and women who possess both attributes, it is rare. Dreamers and doers are generally poles apart in their temperament, their management technique, and their source of motivation.

The *dreamer* is the creative, imaginative, and visionary force. He is the one who is out front of everyone else when it comes to ideas and the future.

The *doer* is the diligent, detailed, production planner who can accomplish the dreamer's vision. To him, the future is somewhere in another zip code. Today's problems are the tasks at hand.

More often than not, there is only one of these forces in true command at the top of most small and medium-sized companies. This leads to a dysfunctional executive branch with no one in authority to tell the top that it is running the race with only one good leg. It's a family with one spouse – functional, but largely inadequate in critical areas of successful operation.

Companies, like families, can function like this for years with marginal success. But the *real stuff* that makes the magic of extraordinary success stays bottled up by the one-legged giant who, in the traditional sense of dysfunction, maintains control of the family using the familiar tools of fear, intimidation, money, power, manipulation, and even disarming charm when necessary.

Studies have been done to determine the rates of success and failure of businesses. Some studies have presented statistical reasons for business failures. A Monthly Labor Review story stated that "Across all sectors, 44 percent [of businesses] survived through the fourth year.... 31 percent to the seventh year.... Individual industries behaved in a similar manner."[1]

An article in the journal Small Business Economics a few years ago referring to Dun & Bradstreet data on business closings stated, "... 76 percent of new firms were open after two years, 47 percent after four years and 38 percent after six years." The writer went on to say "... previous researchers had not distinguished business closures from business failures. They mention that closing firms could have been financially successful but closed for other reasons: the sale of the firm or a personal decision by the owner to accept employment with another firm, to retire, or the like."[2]

In the same journal article, the writer noted that BITS, the Business Information Tracking Series of the U.S. Census Bureau showed that "66 percent of new businesses survive two years or more, 50 percent survive four years or more, and 40 percent survive six years or more."[3]

All of these statistics are roughly consistent in their reporting of business success and failure rates, within reasonable margins for error.

In an online article by Anita Campbell, *New research from the U.S. Bureau of Labor Statistics* suggests that most failures of American startups will occur in the first two years of their existence. After that, the rate of business failure slows.

"The data show that, across sectors, 66 percent of new establishments were still in existence 2 years after their birth, and 44 percent were still in existence 4 years after.... It is not surprising that most of the new establishments disappeared within the first 2 years after their birth, and then only a smaller percentage disappeared in the subsequent 2 years. These survival rates do not vary much by industry."[4]

I recall reading an article a few years ago from the Small Business Administration Office of Advocacy. The article estimated at that time there were roughly six million businesses in the U.S. My notes from that article indicated about eighty percent of those had less than twenty employees and about ten percent had over five hundred employees. That left over six hundred thousand businesses in the mid-range of twenty to five hundred employees. How many of those businesses are still operating?

In many cases financing and cash flow are the key issues in failure.

The Small Business Administration lists reasons for small business failures on their website as lack of experience, insufficient capital, over-investment in fixed assets, poor credit arrangements, and personal use of business funds among other things. They leave out the most critical need in my view: Good management with a mix of *dreamers* and *doers*.

Defining success, like defining failure, can be difficult, but there are thousands of businesses each year that are unsuccessful. Why?

It is my belief that in the majority of failures the problem can be traced back to the day when the original vision began to convert to a comprehensive business plan.

In more cases than not, the dreamer who had the vision also believed they were capable of carrying out that vision using the same mind, gifting, talents, and skills that brought forth the original idea. Thousands upon thousands of businesses never make it past those first critical years because the dreamer thought he was also the doer, or the doer believed that a one-time dream was all it would take to be successful. The idea was too good to fail.

There is a better way to prepare for success. In a world that screams "be all that you can be," I want to encourage you to be smarter than that.

I want you to be realistic. Let's start by swallowing hard and asking the tough questions: What do I bring to the table of this new startup? What are the boundaries of my abilities?

I encourage you to take a candid look at what you have to offer. Be willing to accept your limitations and be ready to delegate to others who are gifted in a way that you are not.

You may need to swallow your pride as you learn to share the responsibilities that will bring success and let you reap the rewards of success that many experts have overlooked.

This book is not the key to your success. I do trust, however, that it will offer you some valuable insights to keys that can help you to humbly and unselfishly surround yourself with others who are gifted in ways you are not. Collectively you can achieve your dream.

CHAPTER ONE

Dreamers, Doers & The Dysfunctional 3-Ts

Frank was a construction manager with a large construction firm. He was a good man who worked his way up the ladder. He paid his dues. He had worked hard and now, in his early forties, he had reached his goal.

Frank was a dreamer, an idea man, a step ahead of others, and he knew it. He had managed to move up with his own skills which were superior to those around him. He had a proactive personality that kept things moving and everyone energized. He was able to generate excitement for himself and those around him.

He realized early on that he could get others to respond to his ideas and direction. Frank had a way with people.

His company always operated with few problems, and new growth had kept everyone moving onward and upward. Frank, in particular, had benefited from this upward mobility and he relished his role in the company.

He was in a work environment that put to good use the vision, organization, and strategies of the 3-Ts of a successful business:

- teamwork
- territory
- trust.

Frank had tried some side deals along the way. They were small opportunities, and he had made money on some, lost money on others. He knew, deep down, that he was destined for more. He saw himself at the top of his own company one day and he liked the idea.

Birth of a Vision

For months Frank was aware of one area in his industry where there were clear shortcomings that no one was addressing. It seemed to be universal throughout his area of specialization. Recognizing the apparent void in his trade, he knew his idea had value. He was a motivator who believed in his ability to communicate and inspire others to see what he saw.

Using his weekends and evenings, he created a prototype product, labored to refine it, and gave birth to what he knew would be a catalyst to his own new world. With minimum fear and a great idea in hand, he made the break with his employer to finally do his own thing.

He cashed in some stock, gathered his savings, borrowed from his parents and in-laws, and set out to introduce his "new baby" to an industry that needed it. It was a "can't miss" deal. Everybody he had shown it to agreed—this idea had wings.

He began by hiring some key people as his first employees. Money was in the bank for the start up, and a few key sales were made before the door ever opened. The dream was on firm footing.

His mind was racing with variations on his new product. It would easily transpose into another commercial area of the industry, and with the prospects of success looming, Frank could finally begin getting a head start on his future.

Frank couldn't wait to get to his office in the morning. It didn't get any better than this. Life was good.

Death of a Vision

Twenty-two months later it was all over. The last seven months had been a nightmare. Competition had come in a year before. He had run into a serious production problem. There had been personnel issues. Conflicts had developed with two key managers who had become too insistent on changing some of Frank's production schemes and financial projections. This was his baby and neither of these managers understood how important it was to let him, who had been sleeping with this dream for years, carry out the vision that he had birthed.

His dream was becoming his nightmare

His dream was becoming his nightmare of resistant managers, failed production schedules, and regular budget shortages. How many balls could he keep in the air at one time? This is crazy!

Reality now was reduced to weighing options – and they were all negative. He could sell what was left to his competitors. Or he could take personal bankruptcy on his creditors and face ten years of slow payback to his relatives and the IRS payroll tax shortages.

But why? How could it all end like this?

The First "T" — Teamwork

Frank is a prime example of how the 3-Ts of a successful operation and business setting can become dysfunctional.

Frank had a great lineup on the field, even in the coaching positions. The driving force at the top, however, was never a consideration. *He was the top!* Why should that be considered? He had been in this industry for years. He knew it inside and out. And the product was the idea of the decade.

What Frank didn't realize, however, was that he had simply moved the philosophy of business from his previous company and position to his new endeavor –

assuming *he* had everything it took to be all that was needed for success.

But the strategies, positioning, goals and action plans that had filtered down from the top at his previous company were never a real and strategic part of his new venture and vision. He had dreamed big, but he falsely believed that a dream and some industry experience were all he needed to be successful.

The following comparisons show how Frank's new company was dysfunctional in its potential to operate successfully.

PREVIOUS COMPANY	FRANK'S COMPANY
Dreamer & Doer Partners	Dreamer / Frank
▼	▼
Vision & Strategic Plan	Vision / Frank
▼	▼
Field Managers	Manager / Frank
▼	▼
Crew Chiefs / Coaches	Coach / Frank
▼	▼
Ahead of the Curve	Behind the Curve

Frank's team had a void at the top with Frank limited to the dreamer role without an equally authoritative counterpart in a doer role to plan and strategize his vision. This amounted to half of the necessary leadership to successfully launch or grow a sound company. This baby was a potential giant alright, but one that was trying to run with only one leg.

The management structure of his company discouraged the crew chiefs (coaches) and team on the field from ever receiving honest and candid input from Frank. Never fully secure in their positions, there were no avenues of communication available to suggest to him that his solo leadership was incomplete. They couldn't tell the giant he had only one leg. When they tried, Frank's controlling temperament, double-talk, forceful defensiveness, and disarming charm dismissed their messages as naive notions or uninformed suggestions without merit. "Trust me," Frank proclaimed to the end.

The team was competent and continued to produce, doing an above average job. But knowing Frank's boundaries and fearing rejection they never learned to cross the communication threshold. The risk for them was too great. There was no one on the team who dared lead them to confront the one who unknowingly had a death grip on his own dream.

The Second "T" – Territory

Territory is that imaginary boundary that exists within the fabric of every manager's area of responsibility. It's as critical to understand as teamwork.

There are two territories of authority that are essential to the successful operation of a company.

First, the dreamer has the vision to look above the horizon. He sees beyond today. In fact today is, to a large degree, an impatient moment in time holding them back from the reality of what is to come tomorrow.

The doer, on the other hand, has the ability to focus on the tasks at hand today and to clearly determine which tasks need to be accomplished and in what order. Doers naturally manifest their abilities to develop blueprints, procedures, and strategies to give managers the needed directions, goals, and action plans to fulfill those vital tasks necessary to make the vision a reality.

However, seldom do these two qualities of dreaming and doing manifest themselves in the same person. The characteristics of each put them in direct opposition with the very temperament of the person with whom they must team. In later chapters I will discuss the trademarks of each of these types, but suffice it to say now that each has its own territory and although there is overlap, they are nations unto themselves. One without the other is too often failure waiting to happen.

Only 15 percent of an iceberg is seen above the water.

A good visual to understanding this is a side view of an iceberg. Only 15 percent of an iceberg is seen above the water. 85 percent is under the water line.

The same is true of most companies. We see the end product, the advertising, the sales team, and upper management. We seldom see the design, financing, materials, production, and shipping processes at work.

A successful company can be vision driven, but it must also have capable doers with the authority to drive the vision behind the company walls.

The Third "T" – Trust

Understanding the basic need for teamwork and having clearly defined the reality of territorial integrity, the remaining factor for making a successful company is the development of trust between the dreamer and the doers behind the company walls.

Dreamers and doers have vital qualities that will contribute to the success of the company. However, at some point there is a need for trust between the two if they are to make their contributions fully effective.

Trust doesn't come easily, especially at the hands of what are normally very strong-minded individuals.

In a general scenario, trust can be defined as "the firm reliance on the integrity, ability, or character of another person." Frank needed one key individual to work alongside him to help fulfill his vision—a vice president, a chief of staff, a chief operating officer.... in short, a doer, someone with the gifting and skills to make his ideas workable.

Since this is one of the foundation keys in a relationship between the dreamer and the doer, let's look at what makes trust workable.

Merriam-Webster's Online Dictionary defines trust as "assured reliance on the character, ability, strength, or truth of someone or something."

Another way of looking at trust is one in whom confidence and faith has been placed. Just as faith is the currency in the spiritual world, trust is the currency in developing partnerships at the management level of successful companies.

We don't see a great deal about the need for synergism in corporations anymore—the need for all of the people to work not for themselves but for the common good of the team and the company. Our nation was built with a synergistic focus by those who wanted to create something larger than themselves that would benefit all. As we have moved away from that mentality as a nation to the self-serving, narcissistic mindset we have today, we have lost the ability to trust in one another.

In a business setting, lack of trust can create havoc at the top—subtly, silently, destructively. Whether a business is owned and operated by one person or many, there is a need for top management to establish a trust factor that radiates through every sector of the organization. This trust must begin with owners, partners, or top management, and it must have a common belief in the inherent success values of integrity and character.

I have a small, nicely designed art card hanging in my office. It simply states: *"Never compromise your integrity!"* My wife gave it to me as a gesture of support at a time when I was taking a personal stand against what I felt were compromising issues with others with whom I was involved through ownership.

Many would view the differences as minor judgment calls. But in my mind many minor judgment calls have progressively led to the deterioration of values within our society. The gradual deterioration of basic integrity has seeped into our government, our corporations, our institutions of learning, our churches, and our homes. It is an insidious poison that has eaten away at our trust in others and left us with doubts and fears at every level.

Dreamers and Doers

Had Frank recognized the need for a strong doer to complement his dreamer and visionary style of leadership he might have accepted his limitations to successfully develop a strong company model on his own.

If Frank had just known his need for that one key individual, things might have been different. Frank needed help: key individuals that could offer the valuable gifting assets that he lacked.

First, he needed one or two close coworkers or partners who were *doers*—who had the diligent force, understanding, and authority to mix the detailed functions of cost analysis and purchasing with the insight of knowledgeable sales forecasting and personnel needs.

Second, he needed *doers with integrity*—those who were willing to not compromise values for dollars, position, or power.

Thirdly, he needed *doers* with not only the right gifting, but the right temperament to work with him without letting personality conflicts affect the united front for the successful implementation of good business strategies and action plans for the company.

Frank needed desperately to realize his need for *doers* to compliment his visionary skills and to bring balance to his own shortcomings, key people that he could *trust* with his vision and count on to reach the lofty goals that were a part of the dream.

Most people are limited by their gifting, temperament, and natural inclinations.

The lesson we learn from Frank is that most people are limited in their understanding of all the facets of what constitutes success and how to achieve it. They are limited by their gifting, temperament, and natural inclinations as they approach problems and solutions.

In the management consulting work I have done I have been impressed with managers who recognize and accept their limitations and are willing to search outside themselves for guidance and direction.

If a business is too small to have good balance at the top, the owner must be willing to gather one or two accessible advisors who are strong in areas of his weakness. And wisdom would not stop at having them available, but would commit to carrying out their advice—even when it may seem to go against the grain of personal solutions. *Trust* is a choice we make without having all the information we would like to have.

Frank is a good example of a dreamer, the one who can see beyond the task at hand. But Frank, like many entrepreneurs, was short in the areas of being capable of competently implementing good fulfillment and internal management strategies.

In following chapters we'll examine more closely the attributes and weaknesses of both dreamers and doers. This understanding can help us to better complete our ability to reach a successful goal, but it will also help us come to grips with our own inherent weaknesses in the overall management scheme.

CHAPTER TWO

Trademarks of a Dreamer — Visions Beyond

Dreamers come in all shapes and sizes.

They can be highly educated or simply untaught, rational or irrational, sharp or dull, interesting or boring, legalistically honest or blatantly unethical—but one thing they have in common is their ability to see and think beyond the moment.

A few years ago I consulted for several months with a steel fabrication company located in one of our port cities. They had access to a somewhat consistent stream of contract business, and the courts had agreed that they qualified for reorganization through a chapter eleven bankruptcy filing.

The majority stockholder and chief executive officer was type A plus. He controlled with an iron fist, blatant intimidation, and a management style that kept him in a realm that had a disconnect between present-to-past and present-to-future reasoning.

Typical of companies in crisis, everything in the day-to-day operation of this company was immediate with all decisions falling into the paradigm of <u>this</u> day and <u>this</u> hour.

Teamwork, territory, and trust had to become more than an idealistic conversation.

In the stroke of a gavel, as soon as he filed for chapter eleven, his world was turned upside down. Everything had to be accounted for, new business required signed contracts, old buddies could no longer have the verbal deals to which they had become accustomed, production work orders were now monitored and held up to cost accounting systems, and above all, *teamwork*, *territory*, and *trust* had to become more than an idealistic conversation.

Outside financial services were brought in to restructure all of the accounting processes and assure compliance with the courts. Gradually operational responsibilities were turned over to one of the internal managers who had a good grasp of the industry and was more than willing to learn new methods and procedures. Above all, our newly assigned chief operating officer was very aware of his limitations and ready to trust others with both authority and responsibility as he learned the value of teamwork.

Needless to say, the new procedures didn't fit well with the ex-chief of operations and majority stockholder. Resistance began to build and subtle attempts to bypass new procedures were quietly implemented to hold on to old policies. Tentacles of the past were trying to gain back areas of control. The type A dreamer couldn't bring himself to let go of his ways, his power, and his baby. Ultimately, recommendations were made to the courts to require the CEO to take early retirement. In short, he was told to go home. Let others do what must be done if the company was to survive. With great reluctance he honored the court's decision, emptied his office, and retired.

It was never a matter that his visionary talents

were wrong. It was more the reality that he had created a company that wanted to run with the tigers, but was limited to running on one leg. He couldn't keep it up. Changing times, tighter competition, and worn out managers left him trying to keep too many balls in the air. The business required talent and understanding he didn't have, but he was adept at finding ways to cover his shortcomings.

While a *doer* is intent on bringing order and meaning to the activities of the day through effective and productive thinking, planning, and working, so the *dreamer* from the crack of dawn has his or her thoughts, visions, and focus solely on "what can I do today that will cover the necessary needs of operation so I can expand my view of tomorrow?"

The Dreamer

Characteristically, a dreamer has a more forceful underlying temperament than a doer. They are often type A personalities, strong willed and proactive in everything they do.

I have carefully observed the character qualities and weaknesses usually found in dreamers. They are prone to be

talkative	decisive
persuasive	outgoing
risk takers	carefree
impatient	determined
opportunistic	independent
authoritative	confident
controlling	domineering
unemotional	undisciplined.

Dreamers are motivated by definitions of success that are centered on money or power. Most politicians, for example, are dreamers. They have an uncanny ability to put their spin on matters and make points that appear to be in full accord with their personal beliefs on any topic.

One could assess that our nation's financial instability in recent years was an excellent example of men and women in industry, the financial markets, and in congress who had great visions of power and reward, but lacked ability to heed the doer input that required accountability and sound management systems. The credit markets were a train with many engineers but no reliable brakeman.

Politicians are, to a fault, money or power centered. This is evidenced in the United States where the two major parties are consistently split on money/ power issues. Republicans typically work the money angle with their support of issues that lean toward a free market economy, pro business stance, and pandering to the wealthy. Democrats gain and keep much of their power base by implementing social programs, courting unions, catering to the working class, and giving excessive services and benefits to the underprivileged.

Other leadership positions that seem to be heavily made up of dreamers include ministers, actors, salespeople, builders, and entrepreneurs.

Many dreamers, however, are unable to rise above their personal limitations. I have known numerous top sales producers who have the vision and energy to have their own company, but never take that next step. Their problem? They can't cope with letting another person share in making their vision a reality. They often lack the ability to trust, and many live on the edge of truth, often venturing beyond that boundary. It is common for them to become suspect of others.

For too many dreamers, life is a process of going through the motions, but their future is merely "a living" and they will eventually struggle with failure which will manifest itself in defeat and repressed anger. In the sales field particularly they are often counted in the multitude that was represented by the role of Willie Loman in Arthur Miller's marvelous work *Death Of A Salesman*. Willie could only see what should have been. He could never come to grips with his own limitations. As a result he ultimately faced the limitation of life itself—and what could have been.... if only. Tragically, Willie's fate is shared daily by many dreamers in the business world.

Before you conclude that dreamers are tragically inept, think again. We need dreamers. They are the innovators, the creative founts, the initiators, and the imaginative drivers who give us the tenacity and aggressive energy to move to new levels in business and in life. We need them. They are a critical piece in the road to success in a consumer-driven, free-market economy. They are major players on the world stage, and we must recognize the importance of the role they bring to the table.

We must also be willing to recognize that their role needs balance. That balance can come from the other half of this great equation—the doer.

CHAPTER THREE

Trademarks of a Doer — The Task at Hand

Just as dreamers have the inherent ability to visualize great ideas and initiate their start up, so doers have the capacity to direct their intensity and energy toward the task of completion. They are organizers, producers, and detail-driven finishers.

While *dreamers* visualize new possibilities for their original ideas, doers work feverishly to bring the idea under better control.

Doers are generally not comfortable with multiple

tasks, and consequently have a tendency to immerse themselves in individual problems, which gives them better control of the whole.

At a meal with one or two of their favorite foods along with one or two of their less favorite foods, the dreamer will eat the favorite first; the doer will save the best till last. The dreamer just can't wait to taste the best of life. The doer is a plodder and will save the best until last to enhance the joy of finishing well.

An example of how that translates into the affairs of business might have a chief executive officer (dreamer) asking his chief financial officer (doer) for a fourth-quarter expense projection on their chain of *Big Guy Cafeterias*. The dreamer is asking for an average of the previous four quarters along with an educated guess on the effect of any noticeable trends: "Give me a ballpark number so I sound good at my lunch with our banker tomorrow."

To the doer, an educated guess is asking for the near-impossible. Averages and trends are only the tip of the iceberg. He must also consider what days the coming holidays fall on, what the major sporting, concert, and NASCAR events coming into the area are, what the company has booked in parties and banquets, and numerous other issues that can impact the bottom line of the competent and reasonable projection—i.e., "I'm not trained to give educated guesses. Next time give me a head's up."

Don't misunderstand. Both dreamers and doers who are effective in their job need to control. That control is channeled in different directions and through different means.

When not in total control, they feel totally out of control.

Control is an underlying personal issue with both dreamers and doers. *When they do not have total control of a project, they tend to feel totally out of control.*

Because doers are finishers, they visualize individual tasks in their completed state. Thus to throw a new idea into the mix or to re-strategize the goal is a burden with stressors that play directly into *their* control issues.

There are variables and exceptions, but, in general, doers are highly task centered and, more often than not, perfectionists.

Doers are sometimes a confused lot since they live in that no-man's-land of loving the dreamer's ideas, imagination, vision, and ever-evolving fantasy variables, yet hating the threat these bring to their own perfectionistic, completion-focused, "lose-control-and-die" mentality.

The Doer

Some of the traits I have observed in the makeup of a doer:

predictable	deliberate
finisher	organized
modest	humorous
dependable	efficient
loyal	practical
stubborn	perfectionistic
defensive	analytical
critical	indecisive
self-protective	stingy

A few leadership positions that appear to be heavily made up of doers include accountants, teachers, engineers, technicians, musicians, diplomats, and inventors.

A doer is motivated by definitions of success that are centered on money or power—just like the dreamer. The difference is how it is accomplished.

Git 'er Done

Doers have, by nature, a "get it done" mentality. While the dreamer sees opportunities as a part of a maze that stretches across the horizon of tomorrow, the doer sees the same opportunities as problems, creating singular issues which must be conquered one by one. There is nothing more critical than getting into the work at hand and bringing each task to completion.

Interestingly, as the two strengths battle for dominance in the larger framework of the struggle, there is a tendency on the part of both to allow their natural, positive discernment to provoke an unnatural, negative spirit.

The doer knows what it takes to get the job under control and on line for efficient completion. He or she becomes critical of those who do not comprehend the methodical focus that is required if even the immediate goals are not quickly brought under the umbrella of pigeon-hole organization.

The dreamer, on the other hand, is always aware of his or her creative abilities to project and articulate the vision. The tendency is to become overtly critical of those who put up barriers that can slow the process toward the goal.

While the doer's methodical nature is precisely

what the dreamer needs to complete his or her vision, it is also the very attribute that drives their anxiety level to new heights in having to deal with it consistently. In fact, many of the natural assets of the doer are seen as obstacles to the dreamer and vice versa.

For example, I would consider most accountants to be doers. They have an inner drive to bring order to apparent chaos, as well as an inner need to find a place for everything and have everything in its place. Accountants tend to be deliberate, predictable, and completion oriented. Their attention to details, understanding of how certain rules apply to income, expense, balance sheets, and profit and loss statements combined with their overall drive to cause others to "see it their way" are great qualities when properly directed. These attributes can also be great detriments when not balanced by a vision that gives proper meaning to their work of organization.

Positions of authority and leadership require doers to move into expanded roles that can be very uncomfortable to them. However, in ownership and key management positions, doers must learn to enlarge their acceptance of the vision, as well as the visionary, and give themselves the freedom to allow today's tasks to stay open ended.

Admittedly, it can be difficult for doers to move

into the unknown where they permit free thinkers to move into their perfectionistic environment. Perhaps an even greater challenge is simply learning to allow themselves a good night's sleep in the middle of what appears to them as confusion and chaos.

CHAPTER FOUR

The Appearance of a Coming Struggle

Somewhere in the subconscious thinking of our dreamer and our doer is a battle that periodically comes to the surface. The deep-seated desire for success and achievement is inevitably frustrated by their personal limitations. In that moment the dreamer sees that he or she needs a doer, and the doer unable to see the dream unfold is thus confronted with his or her need for a dreamer.

But in the midst of this battle there is an ever-present denial system at work. It's a twenty-four hour law that can't be surgically removed. Call it pride, maybe independence, but it's always calling.

Pride is an ego-based drive that goes measurably beyond what we prefer to think of as *confidence.* Pride is usually very deceptive—even destructive—when it breeds a form of self-centeredness in search of an independent and selfish fulfillment. Several centuries ago John Donne, the English poet, expressed his conclusion that "...no man is an island, entire of itself."

To be sure, there can be a positive side to pride, a side that sees achievement only in retrospect—a view that what was not, now is! And coupled with the gracious recognition of their part in the accomplishment it becomes a pride that is nicely blended with genuine humility.

An Operational Perspective

Making the assumption that, at some point, our dreamer recognizes the need for a doer and our doer sees the lack of vision in his or her plan, let's now take the next step and place both into our operational perspective.

The doer may have brought in a top sales and marketing driver to enhance sound development for the service or product.

Our dreamer, seeing the need for better organizational structure, defined goals, and growth strategies, also takes a major step of bringing in a key employee. Many small businesses are literal "mom and pop" operations, growing out of the dreams of a husband and wife who have talked, visualized, fantasized, and ached for the day the dream morphed into a reality.

But whatever the makeup of ownership, the stage is now set for potential battle, as the forces are in place.

The "My Way" Dance

There is a broad and basic philosophical difference in the dreamer and doer approach to operational philosophy. There is a marked distinction in what each perceives is needed to be the driving force toward the future.

This difference sets the stage for the infighting that can bring severe strain into the relationship and reduce the ability to work toward that singular purpose and goal.

They began their venture with a need and respect for each other's ability to contribute toward their combined singleness of purpose. But danger can be lurking. That unity can be lost along the way because of an inability and unwillingness to see the impact of their philosophical differences and their individual gifting upon the larger view of how to achieve their goals.

The Dreamer's Personality

Basic to the dreamers natural business acumen and strategy is the gift to influence others with dreams, ideas, and vision. This is most likely what attracted the doer to the dreamer in the first place.

Dreamers have the ability to convince others....

The dreamer has the ability to convince others that the dream has the potential to successfully impact all who have the foresight to engage its vision.

The reality of the moment, however, is that what the listener is buying into is the dreamer, not the dream. And out of that transaction comes the foundation for a personality driven venture: "Upon my vision

I will build the company."

The doer, on the other hand, may be a social bore, provide a snobbish insight to intellectually stimulating views of life, and capture the interest of all in his midst with his gentle stability and warm humor. One attribute is certain, and that is his or her ability to clearly see the task at hand and bring closure in a methodical and timely fashion.

Doers are generally more focused than dreamers. They are wrapped in the moment, the process. It is difficult for a doer to jump ahead and read the last page of a book because they know and respect the detail and diligence that were woven together to give substance to the whole. Although they have great compassion and respect for the writer, they see the author as an instrument in the creative process. The process itself commands their intensity and focus. *Upon a systematic process we will build the company.*

The Wedge

Early on in the business relationship all seems to go well. There are flashes of jockeying for position as discussions lead to decisions and differing methods of operation fall into place.

Occasional disagreements occur but seem to find resolution without the loss of authority for either party. Yet, ever so subtly over weeks and months, the control issues in their personalities, wrapped in the universal law of pride and independence, begin to slide into the relational environment.

The dreamer is learning that his or her forceful personality can be effective in manipulating the decision-making process when there is disagreement.

Conversely, the doer becomes aware that he or she seems to compromise more than the dreamer in matters of decision. With this awareness comes the need to effectively bypass the normal decision-making process by bringing issues, which warrant personal decisive actions, into his or her area of responsibility.

On the surface everything may look healthy in our company. But the roots of unrest grow, continually watered by the law of pride reaching now into the structure of relationships, vision, and activity.

The wedge of distrust creates its own momentum and subtly joins the underlying need for control.

The wedge is driven deeper into the relationship and subtly the battle is joined.

This struggle for control and independence is a battle neither side really desires. After all, the prospects for success are excellent. The future is bright.

The prospects on the horizon are well above average. Along the way attempts are made to recognize the struggle. Signs of a willingness to reach beyond the struggle appear. There is also an inner force that is just beyond reach. How many times can that inner force be overcome?

CHAPTER FIVE

Forces That Drive the Wedge

There are three destructive forces that threaten to split apart many companies—especially at the top. They may be clothed in a variety of forms and agendas, but they're based on pride, greed, and control.

They arrive subtly and work seductively, but they inevitably come. At one point or another, everyone in upper management, or part of the family in a family–owned business will have to deal with them in the business culture.

Corporate leadership, in particular, must be aware of the power of these negative forces. We must also face the reality that these forces are a part of the basic nature with which we come into this world. And as much as we would like to think of ourselves as being above these energies, an honest appraisal of our own motives in certain situations will reveal the forces at work in our own lives.

Pride

The American Heritage Dictionary / Thesaurus defines pride as "a regarding of oneself with undue favor— i.e. ego, vanity, conceit, narcissism, arrogance, haughtiness, lordliness."

As stated previously, pride isn't always a negative force. Indeed it is an attribute that can be properly channeled to provide a positive motivation.

It is good to have pride in our work, a job well done, or efforts to strive for excellence, but it can also become a force that drives people apart. It can take a unified group of people moving toward an ultimate goal and create an environment of division, control, and distorted beliefs.

When many companies begin, they experience a

leadership that is both capable and willing to put pride aside to join a team committed to pulling together toward a common purpose.

However, pride is subtle and it manifests itself in a territorial way. For several months I worked to set up a company that was in the van conversion business. We had an arrangement with a national company to run the plant. Our primary purpose was bringing materials in for assembly and completion. At the same time we focused on sales and distribution to eleven eastern states.

Everyone worked together from the start—purchasing, receiving, assembly, sales, distribution, delivery, receivables, and warranty. As time passed, I could see key people and managers becoming more and more territorial. As problems surfaced, there was the natural tendency to cover yourself, to find fault with another department, supplier, or sometimes even a customer. Personality conflicts became more apparent and the blame game became a part of nearly every meeting.

In new businesses during the first months, the hardships, pressures, and demands of any organization may be enough to keep pride in check. But as differences become known, joint decisions have to be made through compromise, and tendencies develop that can carry subtle resentments.

Suddenly, what is commonly referred to as the teeter-totter principle begins to show in relationships. We create ways to put other people's actions in a *down* perspective so that we push our own views *up* through comparative association.

The teeter-totter principle puts others down to raise us up.

On a Scale of 'Me' — I'm a 10

We all have good balance in our own eyes. But one of the most selfless acts we can perform for our organization is to seriously consider other viewpoints. It is an even more fruitful exercise if we can learn to look objectively at other people's perspectives as more than just opinions. Learning to look beyond words to personal views can often lead to ideas and thought-starters that can impact our own decision making process.

I've been involved in organizations where in

order for new ideas to be accepted—especially those generated at a lower level—it was imperative that they be presented to the company heads in such a way that the company heads ultimately could take credit for the idea. If it wasn't presented so as to come out the other side of the meeting as a leadership idea, it was destined for failure. Consequently, there was an ongoing manipulation of ideas, rather than an open exchange of concepts and thoughts.

The world is filled with leaders who steal the ideas of others to feed their own advancement and ego. Sadly, companies are filled with those who let them do

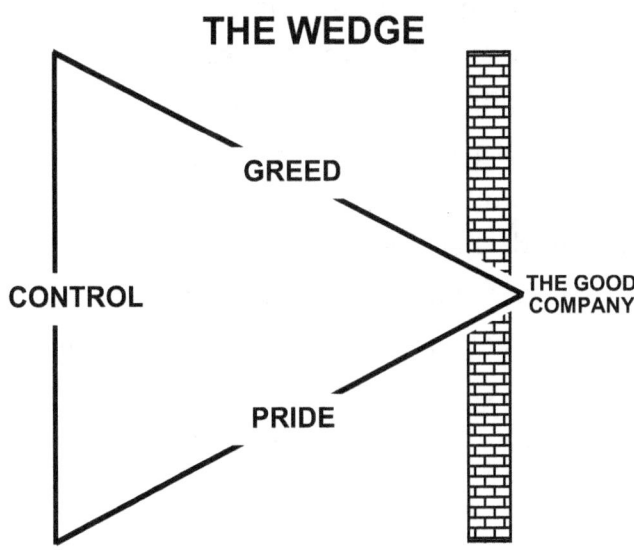

THE WEDGE

GREED

CONTROL

THE GOOD
COMPANY

PRIDE

it. The false belief systems become part of the momentum of the wedge.

In the example I made reference to, it was vital to stop the territorialism before it created major divisions. My first move was to determine who was working well together and where the conflicts were surfacing. Getting to know each individual was important, to better understand their personality and their temperament (covered in more detail in the following chapter). My goal was to encourage those who worked together and to help them to better understand the pitfalls of "the wedge."

At the same time I met individually with those who appeared to be developing conflicts and protecting territory. My goal was to gently help them see their way around the conflict issues and to make a connection with the idea of synergy and the advantages of focusing on the larger picture. In that process we discussed their temperament, those things that blocked them from making better choices, and even elements in their beliefs about corporate culture that worked against a more peaceful environment in which they could blossom and move up the corporate ladder.

Greed

Another area that the top of every company needs to deal with is greed if they are to set an example that will make a difference at mid-management and field levels.

Most employees don't have a problem watching their owners, leaders, and managers make money for the company and for themselves. But *greed is an attitude* that works itself out into deceitful forms of behavior. It slowly but surely takes its toll as it drives the wedge deeper and deeper into the heart of the company.

I am not suggesting that we negate our basic profit-generating goals. We should all get excited about a new company or product that can become a cash cow and produce above-average profitability. Greed, however, is taking sound fiscal principles and perverting them into a prevailing attitude that soon is felt at all levels of a company.

Consider a salesman who is doing a great job for his company in a position to impact the success of his company and affect the company's profitability— and his own income. The line between greed and healthy negotiating can soon become vague and distorted. Greed can become a factor in the negotiations, and a win/lose attitude will soon develop. In that kind of scenario the deal must be manipulated so that the salesman is the winner and his customer the loser rather than holding to an effort to reach a win/win deal where both parties can walk away winners. Not only will win/win lead to an end result that is positive for both sides, but the salesman has made a friend rather than an enemy and the long-term gains from that will be advantageous for him and the company. Integrity is established as a part of both personal and corporate image and culture.

Control

The final side on the wedge is control. Control is power. It is a subtle motivating force that results in an attitude of power more than teamwork and single-ness of purpose. Control can be a negative force that can work against everything that is good for a company.

Regardless of whether you are an office worker or the owner of the company, power is something that comes with position. It is only bad when it is *misused*.

In some companies even the lowliest of employ-ees can develop a power base by cornering the control of product or vital information. The now famous adage "Information is power" does have a sense of entitlement. Those who have the information have an element of power over those who do not. That is also what drives much of the gossip in an office environment—holding onto information for the sake of power.

Our study of dreamers and doers reveals that doers will strive toward more subtle areas of power. They will have control of the books, the inventory, the personnel, or the information that the dreamer does not have. They can use that as a power base to get the things they want, even if that one thing is to share the control.

Dreamers, on the other hand, can go out into the marketplace and use the information gleaned about new products or services to create their own islands of power and so gain a notch up on the doer.

Power bases can and do bring conflict into a company at every level. The sad but true story is that such maneuvering goes on everywhere.

The Full Wedge

Pride, greed, control—together they can form a triangle of destruction for any company or business. At best, they develop an undercurrent of confusion at every level. At worst, they drive competent people from their jobs and destructively eat away at the fabric of a company's integrity and strength.

Pride is a law.
Greed is an attitude.
Control is a hammer.

Pride is a law. Greed is an attitude. Control is a hammer. *The misuse of all three is a choice.* This three-sided wedge of poison leaves a path of distrust wherever it goes.

It Ain't Necessarily So

It is not an absolute law that the wedge be a decisive factor in every company. It is an absolute law, however, that it will be hovering to seek an open door in every area of operation—starting at the top.

One very simple adjustment in the paradigm of business culture can disarm all three of these forces. The wedge can be diffused.

Stay with me! The best is yet to come.

CHAPTER SIX

The Secret
of Temperaments

I want to take the reader a different direction for a glimpse at the underlying drives that are a vital part of the human condition and more than apparent in nearly every workplace.

The corporate ranks are filled with men and women who are dreamers and doers, as well as those unique individuals who carry enough of both qualities to be known as dreamer/doer combinations.

Successful leaders are found in each of the three

categories. I want to offer a brief effort to convey how these temperaments work in the marketplace and how negative discrepancies can be overcome.

These concepts will help you understand what drives a dreamer or doer to think and act like they do under working circumstances. Understanding the person's primary and secondary temperament is a major step toward understanding why that person's strengths and weaknesses are a major part of the mix we refer to as the company culture—an internal system and attitude that filters down to all levels of individuals that make up the company roster.

Leaders Develop

To select a few national figures might help us understand the relationship between dreamers, doers, and our basic temperaments.

Certainly men like Lee Iacocca, the ex-head of Chrysler could be described as a dreamer. Bill Gates, Billy Graham, and Ronald Reagan could be classified as dreamers - men who could visualize what could be.

Those we can likely identify as doers might be a General Eisenhower or Patton, a president's chief of staff or most members of any professional sports team. Although they usually get involved in someone else's dream, they have an inherent quality that lets them see not just the dream, but, more clearly, the path to the fulfillment of the dream. They foresee the ditches and roadblocks, as well as the directional markers that lead to the dream.

Finally, there are those who have a combined ability to be classified as both dreamers and doers. One of these is Herb Kelleher, who successfully organized and for many years ran Southwest Airlines. It was not unusual to see Kelleher behind the desk at an airport taking tickets, greeting people, and encouraging his workers. He could dream and do. Steve Jobs of Apple Computer also falls into this category of a dual leadership role.

Temperaments Are Fixed

Dictionary.com describes temperament as "the combination of mental, physical, and emotional traits of a person; natural predisposition, unusual personal attitude or nature as manifested by peculiarities of feeling, temper, action, etc., often with a disinclination to submit to conventional rules or restraints."

The reference to "natural disposition" is key.

Every human being comes into this world with a natural predisposition. Certainly parents, environment, peers, and experiences have an impact on our personality, our thinking, our beliefs, and our decision making. But there is a river in each of us that never changes. It carries that "natural disposition," the "unusual personal attitude or nature" that dictionaries refer to.

I have four children. Early in their young lives we could see their natural disposition on display. As adults, that same temperament is still very apparent in everything they do.

Temperaments are not a recent discovery. As early as 400 B.C. Hippocrates, the father of medicine, distinguished the four temperaments. There are many variations of how the four are identified and named. Some separate them by animals, others by colors, but the essence is the same.

The German philosopher Immanuel Kant popularized them in Europe in the late 1700's. A general condensation of his consensus would be

> **Sanguine**—carefree and full of hope.
> Sociable, takes nothing too seriously. Easily
> fatigues and bored by work. Seldom
> persistent.
> **Choleric**—competitive and quickly roused.

Loves to see the opponent give in. Good at giving direction, loves open recognition and loves pomp and formality. Lots of pride and self-love.

Melancholy—highly focused, gives ultimate value to everything that concerns them. Finds every cause for anxiety. Suspicious, concerned.... but thoughtful.

Phlegmatic—lacks expressive passion. Moves neither quickly nor easily. Acts on principle, has balance and strong values.

Every business owner should understand the differences in temperaments

Every business owner and manager should understand the differences in temperaments. This is a vital part of a person's makeup, and a good manager will be better able to work with, assign, set goals for, and understand his people if he better understands their natural disposition.

Specifics on the Temperaments

There are many books written on the temperaments. In a somewhat condensed format I'd like to offer the reader a brief insight to the major differences in the temperaments.

Although everyone generally has a primary temperament, it is not unusual to have a very strong secondary temperament.

As an example, my primary is that of a phlegmatic, but I have a strong secondary choleric temperament. In a practical sense I am phlegmatic in my home and personal life, but the choleric comes out in my business and career areas.

As you read through the following descriptions of each temperament, put a check by those words that you feel best describe you. Total each category, then read back through my narrative on your highest total. This condensed version is not foolproof, but it can serve to give you a glimpse of where your strengths lie as well as point out the weaknesses you must work to improve and/or avoid.

As you understand the temperaments, it should be easy to see how their natural inclinations play into the mentality of the dreamer and the doer.

Sanguine

The sanguine is popular, personable and capable of enjoying life and other people. They are often naive, deer-in-the-headlights responsive, very talkative and expressive, and always curious and questioning of others.

Here are some words that describe the sanguine:
energetic
cheerful
believable
captivating
expressive
disorganized
distracted
fickle
lively
boisterous
messy
frank
expectant
permissive
flirtatious
popular
active
outgoing

spirited

impulsive

gabby

undisciplined

temperamental

Some of the fields that are well suited to the Sanguine are

sales, sales, sales

hosts/hostesses

receptionists

actors

conference leaders/speakers

The sanguine will usually fall into the dreamer group since they are outgoing and friendly to all who come their way. They are naturals in a sales career and, like the choleric, can't be bothered with too many details.

Choleric

The choleric is a born leader, strong willed, active, practical, and generally stubborn. The choleric enjoys opposition and a challenge, loves an emergency, and has an organized mind. They consider meetings, details, and social events a waste of time.

Here are some words that describe the choleric:
daring
argumentative
resolute
domineering
competitive
confident
gutsy
decisive
commanding
impatient
freewheeling
intolerant
leader
direct
influential
productive
proud
frank
unyielding
self-contained
strong-willed
stubborn
brash

A few of the fields that are well suited to the choleric are

contractors/developers
entrepreneurs
chief executive officers
politicians
professional athletes
military leaders

Cholerics generally fall into the dreamer category since they are focused on what can be and are prone to be bored with too many details.

Melancholy

Intellectual, genius, gifted, talented, and creative are words that often describe the Melancholy. Research analysts, musicians, and philosophers come from this category. The other side of their creativity however, is a very moody person who can be perfectionistic and overdone on details.

Here are words that describe the melancholy
analytical
shy
considerate
cultured
particular
exacting

idealistic

unassured

introvert

faithful

moody

organized

methodical

determined

pessimistic

planner

unsociable

respectful

self-sacrificing

perceptive

leery

thoughtful

remote

A few of the fields where the melancholy is often seen are

artists/musicians

scientists/doctors

professors

theologians

engineers/craftsmen

The melancholy, although often suited to the fringes of the dreamer mentality, will usually fall into the doer group. Their methodical, planner, and organized skills strongly help them to follow through the dream committed to getting the work done.

Phlegmatic

The phlegmatic is easy going, a good friend, problem solver, and usually has a great sense of humor. The phlegmatic reminds us that the ground is level no matter who others might think they are. They are always cool and in control and are good at listening and helping.

Here are words that describe the phlegmatic:

adaptable
balanced
negotiable
stable
contented
reserved
diplomatic
friendly
doubting
indecisive
indifferent
mediator

forbearing

forgiving

pleasant

cautious

peaceable

sympathetic

humble

gentle

composed

neutral

consistent

Career fields that are well suited to the phlegmatic are

financial planners

administrators

counselor/therapists

supervisors

negotiator/mediators

Phlegmatics come with a natural doer drive and mentality. Although they are often not grand self-starters, they are the plodders who will see it through to the end.

A Sampling of the Temperaments

I have occasionally taught a course at a local university in addition to being an occasional conference speaker. I have become accustomed to the natural responses of each of the temperament types in the class at the conclusion of any particular session. I can plan on the following:

- A choleric will boldly come to the front to tell me what they think and what they have done to confirm a specific point I made.
- A sanguine tells me they can't wait to tell a friend how they will put to work what they learned today.
- A melancholy will stay in their seat, analyzing, exploring, and becoming more aware of their personal weaknesses.
- A phlegmatic - well, why stand in line to make a point. And frankly, who cares anyway.

Ah, the beauty of the skills, giftedness, and shortcomings of the four temperaments. Yet when placed in their proper roles, these are the dreamers who can dream the practical roads to success, and the doers who, given the freedom, can make it happen.

One without the other is incomplete.

CHAPTER SEVEN

The Cost of Trading Swords for Plowshares

The sword symbolizes a tool for war and destruction. The plowshare is a symbol of a creative unity or yoking together that benefits all.

The wedge is like a sword creating conflict and infighting. Left to its own it will become destructive.

Both the dreamer and the doer have great capacity to identify and counter the effects of the wedge if they are willing to work together in an effort to develop a company culture that has, as its center, the sum of all its parts.

Individually the high cost of giving up the sword of infighting is in finding the willingness to pay the price of always having our own way. It is tragic within the corporate world to find so many insecure people who struggle so in their personal identity that they must rise to a level of position and power to feel good about themselves. And in rising to that level, many often forsake their ultimate success in order to gain absolute control of their own perceived destiny.

Insecure people struggle for position and power in order to feel good about themselves.

The battle cannot be won; it is a matter of resigning to the process of *giving up* the false gratification received from pride, greed, and control and trading up for the true and abiding goals of integrity, cooperation, teamwork, and respect for others.

The Synergism of Trusting Others

Synergism is a resulting power that comes from the trade- offs just described. The *American Heritage Dictionary* defines synergism as "The interaction of two or more agents or forces so that their combined effect is greater than the sum of their individual effects"—and—"Cooperative interaction among groups, especially among the acquired subsidiaries or merged parts of a corporation, that creates an enhanced combined effect."

The cost of synergism does not mean that you or I, as a dreamer or doer, must give up who we are or any part of our identity, talents, gifts, or personal uniqueness. It does require that we choose to value the combined goals that we believe in as more important than our individual need for control. It also requires that we learn to moderate that inherent drive of greed and control.

Some might say "That thwarts the competitive drive through which many succeed." We can view the principle in that way, of course. But it is more important to see that by saying no to some of those inner drives to control others we are saying yes to a team goal that is more achievable, rewarding, and complete. It will, in the end, bring us a more positive power with monetary rewards and achievement. It also brings a more satisfying and less stressful way of goal achievement that money and control can never buy.

Allowing the greater good of the organization's goals to conquer the destructive forces can be a delight to our inner person — and it is that person that we must learn to live with and be at peace with for the remainder of our life.

The goal of becoming a self-made person at the cost of other people's blood is the carryover of the killer instinct mentality that has epitomized the last half of this century in America.

Will it cost us? Of course it will. But it is right! What will it cost? Above all, a strong commitment to a learning process. It is learning to balance our individual rights with our individual responsibilities, and learning to balance our own knowledge with the knowledge of others working toward a single goal. It is agreeing to make our common enemies greed, destructive power, and selfish pride. And, it is agreeing to make our common friends integrity, cooperation, teamwork, and respect for others.

How do you begin? First we must lay a foundation.

Laying the Foundation

I stated earlier that one very simple adjustment in your attitude can, by itself, disarm the wedge. That simple adjustment is well defined in a single word, but it is a hard-learned attitude of heart. It is *humility*.

"But that is for the weak, the wimps," you counter. No, it is only for those who are strong enough to trust its power.

What is humility? Humility is behavior that is unpretentious in attitude and not arrogant or prideful.

Is this a new idea? Not at all. Nearly 3,000 years ago King Solomon wrote that "It is better to be poor and humble than proud and rich. Pride ends in a fall, while humility brings honor."

Humility is an attitude that sets the stage for teamwork whether you're a dreamer or a doer. And the teamwork concept that the ownership and management of any company sets is an example for all who work under its umbrella.

It begins with commitment and will only succeed if we work to keep commitment at the center of the humility principle: commitment to each other and commitment to our common goals.

In the business world humility is getting to know

one another. Whether the people at the top are two partners or a corporate management team, informal personal interaction is key to the work of humility and to the establishment of integrity between one another. If that means a half day a week together on the golf course, a monthly fishing venture, or a relaxed early dinner together every other week with no particular agenda – whatever it is that brings you together to learn more about each other, to communicate at a personal level, and to take your relationships beyond the realm of the normal organizational drives and conflicts – it can be a time of immense value to the overall corporate culture and stability.

It is in these casual environments that we learn to get past our differences in management styles, our disturbing idiosyncrasies and even the differences in our common goals. We learn in all of this to temper our perspectives to include as valid and valuable the views of those we come to know and trust. It is only in this way that we can learn to view the larger goals through similar grids, because we have gotten past the personal insecurities that lock us into the competitive personal battles that tend to place restrictions on our future.

Many companies are shackled from achieving their goals by the invisible chains that keep the individuals at the top from moving forcefully ahead in an environment of unity of purpose through humility and a generous trust of others.

Victors or Victims?

There is a very simple answer for those partners and coworkers who are secure with their own self-worth. It is the authorization of a third party, inside or outside the company, to be given the authority and responsibility to keep a constant watch for any appearance of the three-sided wedge. This person would have the capacity and commitment to blow the whistle on anyone in the ivory tower.

I would call this person a corporate facilitator. Ideally, this facilitator would have daily or near-daily access to both the dreamer and the doer and be able, at any time, to bring their observations to the table. The underlying character quality of humility must be a part of dreamer and doer, as well as facilitator. The net results in the lives of all would be like a breath of fresh air flowing through every area and level of operation. Such a relationship would become a powerful force within any company, ultimately crystallizing the vision and empowering the work force.

The Power of Unity

There is enormous power in unity. That power transcends our mental capacity for knowledge and our personal ability to influence others. All the drive one can muster for a given year cannot compare to the power that is generated by individuals combining their thoughts, emotional strengths, and oneness of spirit toward a common goal—committed to deny their own selfish ambitions for the sake of the common goals, realizing that within their achievement will be rewards for all beyond even their most extravagant desires.

Does this mean we must give up our competitive strengths and the ability to achieve personal goals? Of course not. That is an integral part of our American way of exercising our freedom to become what we dream of becoming. It is more a change of attitude that allows us to be a part of a larger total success rather than striving for personal achievement at the expense of others.

It begins with the reality that dreamers must be allowed to dream, create, risk, and fantasize. And doers must be allowed to do, organize, apply the brakes, and bring the fantasies to earth and achievable practicality.

It's agreeing to put away the swords of territorialism and control and to pick up the plowshare of cooperation, accepting that their greatest contribution toward success is an ability to do "my part." Not the whole, but my part. And do my part well.

A Final Note

It is my hope that this little book will help you understand some of the "why?" reasoning that takes place behind the company walls.

An awareness of the wedge and its seamy friends—pride, greed, and control—is a necessity for sound management. Couple that with a better understanding of some of the inherent tendencies and perspectives that drive the natural disposition of each member of the human family, and you will be in a much stronger position to get your head around the issues that can be destructive within an organization.

The Last Straw

The process would not be complete without first taking a candid look at yourself.

As previously mentioned, humility is one of the great foundation stones of success in every individual and can be the most rewarding of the virtues.

Certainly the business world is filled with the multitudes who think success is money and power. But those are also the people who, when they let down their guard, are the first to confess the emptiness of their success.

I strongly encourage leaders and managers to periodically schedule a day away from it all. Find an isolated and quiet place next to a stream or in a beautiful countryside and give yourself an honest checkup. Build a checklist of strengths and weaknesses.

Above all—never be afraid of the truth.

A Personal Checkup

1. Confront the pride, the greed, the control issues.

_____

_____

_____

_____

_____

_____

2. Just what does humility mean to you?

_____

_____

_____

_____

_____

3. Are you part of the wedge, or do you have the makings for a sound and durable foundation?

_____

_____

_____

_____

_____

4. What is your primary and secondary temperament?

_____

_____

_____

_____

5. What are the strengths of your temperament?

_____

_____

_____

6. Can you honestly identify with the weaknesses of your temperament?

_____

_____

_____

_____

7. What is the primary motivation in your life?

_____

_____

_____

_____

_____

8. Do you believe synergism is an effective concept?

_____

_____

_____

_____

9. Are you ready to pay the price for real, lasting success?

_____

_____

_____

_____

_____

_____

_____

Notes
&
Recommended
Reading

INTRODUCTION

1   *Business Employment Dynamics Data: Survival and Longevity, II*, by Amy E. Knaup and Merissa C. Piazza, Monthly Labor Review, vol. 30, no. 9 (Sept. 2007), pp. 4

2   *Redefining Business Success: Distinguishing Between Closure and Failure* by Brian Headd, Small Business Economics, vol. 21, no. 1 (August 2003), pp. 52-54

3   Ibid

4   *Small Business Trends, Business Failure Rates Highest in First Two Years,* Anita Campbell - http://smallbiztrends.com/2005/07/ business-failure-rates-highest-in.html

CHAPTER SIX - RECOMMENDED READING

1   *Personality Plus*, by Florence Littauer
     Author and Conference Speaker
     Available at http://www.amazon.com/

2   *Transformed Temperaments*,by Tim Lahaye
     Co-Author of the Left Behind Series
     Available at http://www.amazon.com/

Roger Alliman, M.A. has been active as a professional counselor, business executive, adjunct professor, certified mediator, and conference speaker. He has consulted with numerous organizations in need of startup structuring, management stabilization, and reorganization through chapter eleven bankruptcy.